Tools for Kids

Your help handbook with fun exercises, activities and tools to help children to self-regulate and increase their skills

Angie Turner

true, fair and accurate unless the work is expressly described as a work of fiction. Regardless of the nature of this work, the Publisher is exempt from any responsibility of actions taken by the reader in conjunction with this work. The Publisher acknowledges that the reader acts of their own accord and releases the author and Publisher of any responsibility for the observance of tips, advice, counsel, strategies and techniques that may be offered in this volume.

Table of Contents

Introduction

Congratulations on purchasing *ADHD - Tools for Kids,* and thank you for doing so.

I'm Angie Turner, tutor for children with learning disabilities and in the following chapters will discussall that you need to know about parenting a child with ADHD, which is the acronym for Attention Deficit Hyperactivity Disorder. Among all other problems, ADHD is very common in children and it is a type of neurodevelopmental disorder. In some cases, the problem can remain in the child even when he/she has become an adult. Every sphere of the child's life is affected because of this problem, be it friendship, home, or school. The kids struggle with the most basic things of life like sitting still, paying attention to something, or even practicing self-control. Sometimes, children suffering from ADHD show an excessive amount of energy which often turns out to be destructive.

Every parent should be aware of what ADHD is so that they can identify whether their child has this problem or not. The more you learn about it, the more you will know what it entails for your child. In this book, I have included all the information that you will need to help your child move forward in life and guide them well so that they can overcome their problem. As you go through the chapters of this book, you will soon realize that you are not dealing with a lifelong disorder and that it is more like a personality problem and not a medical condition.

There are plenty of books on this subject on the market, thanks again for choosing this one! Every effort was made to ensure it is full of as much useful information as possible, please enjoy!

What Is ADHD?

Do you think that your child has ADHD, but you just can't be sure about it? Well, then you are in the right place because, in this chapter, we are going to discuss what ADHD is and how you will know that your child is suffering from it. If your child has trouble controlling his/her impulses and is mostly hyperactive at all times, then they are probably suffering from ADHD but there are lots of other symptoms to look out for as well. ADHD is not that much common in girls as much as it is in boys. When ADHD continues into adulthood, a person can easily give into addiction, have problems in their relationships, or even have very low self-esteem. Read on to find out more about this neurodevelopmental disorder.

Causes of ADHD

Before we move on to discuss the symptoms of ADHD, let me first give you a brief idea on what causes this problem in the first place. There are several factors that play a role, but most researchers suggest that ADHD is mainly a genetic disorder at its core. There is a part of your brain that is very specifically responsible for the 'executive functioning,' and when a child has ADHD, that part of the brain is affected. This is the reason why children suffering from this problem are unable to show the right emotions, evaluate their behaviors, plan for their future, solve problems, or control their impulses.

The several challenges that are created in a family because of the condition of ADHD can often lead you to forget the facts. The problem, if escalated, affects the child's classroom behavior and his/her personal relationships as well. Some parents are even led to believe that the problem occurred because there was some problem in their style of parenting. Sometimes, people also assume that ADHD is a problem that is triggered by some kind of traumatic activity that happened in the child's early years or any stressful event that they were subjected to. Teachers, who do not understand the gravity of the problem, often label the student as disobedient or lazy.

But, if you truly want to help a person, be it a child or adult, who is suffering from ADHD, you have to start by understanding what the origin of this neurodevelopmental disorder is. Genetic factors are definitely one of the major reasons behind ADHD, but you have to keep in mind that the blame for a child suffering from ADHD does not necessarily have to be put on the parents because they really didn't have anything to do with it.

Heredity

There are so many parents who have this question – whether ADHD is hereditary or not. Well, the answer is yes, it is hereditary. It is typically a disease that runs in families. For the past thirty years, so many types of research are going on to find out more about ADHD. If we are to keep a count, then there are more than 2,000 studies that have been performed to date, and they are still ongoing to truly understand the character of this disorder. Geneticists, psychiatrists, and psychologists have all worked on this disorder. Most of the time, you will see that if a child has ADHD, someone from the child's family – either a parent or any other blood relative – must have had ADHD too.

Several genes have also been identified, and they are most likely to be associated with the problem of ADHD. But in order to specify the exact genetic markers, more studies have to be performed on this subject and if you consider what is found until now, it is believed that more than one gene is involved in this. But you should also know this that there are no genetic tests in relation to ADHD that have been discovered.

You should also not misunderstand this because even if your child has a genetic risk of developing ADHD, it doesn't mean that he/she is definitely going to have it. There are cases where kids did not have ADHD despite having it in their family, and there are cases where kids had ADHD even when none of their family members suffered from it. Because of the hereditary link of ADHD, there are some parents who even feel guilty for it because they think it was them who passed on the problem to their child.

In fact, it has been found that when a family has a child with ADHD, 25% of the relatives of that same family also have shown symptoms of the problem. This rate is way higher when compared to a family that did not have a child with ADHD. Also, if someone has identical twins and one of them already has ADHD, then the chances of the other one having ADHD are 82%. The percentage drops to 38% in the case of fraternal twins and so all of these stats together show what a close link ADHD has with that of genetics.

Brain Anatomy

More and more research has been going on to figure out how ADHD is related to brain structure. It has already been found that in kids, there are certain parts of the brain that do not develop as fast as the others, But by saying this, I do not mean that kids with ADHD are not smart or not talented. It is simply that some part of their brain takes a bit longer to become fully developed. Now, some of these structures play an indispensable role in the case of working memory and emotional control. That is why the self-management system of the brain suffers. But by the time the child reaches adulthood, these structures often undergo change and attain their fully developed stage.

What you have to understand is that the functioning of the brain is somewhat similar to shifting gears. All the parts have to work in unison in order for you to read or write. Neurons are the structures that are responsible for connecting the different cells in the brain. And when a child is suffering from ADHD, it is these neural networks that take longer to develop. One of those neural networks is responsible for making the child come to a resting phase, and it is known as the 'default mode network.' But when children suffer from ADHD, they cannot focus properly because this default mode network takes longer to put other aspects to rest.

Another pathway that is affected is the frontoparietal network, and it is basically responsible for a child's ability to learn new things and make decisions.

Other Factors

In some cases, ADHD can also be caused when the child has suffered some kind of head injury in the childhood phase. Certain prenatal exposures are also harmful to the child and lead to ADHD. These exposures include nicotine and alcohol. And there are certain rare cases where ADHD happens due to environmental reasons. One such example is when a child is exposed to lead, and it leads to stunted development and abnormal behavior.

Symptoms in Children

Like I have told you before, the main symptom of any child suffering from ADHD is that they display a hyperactive and impulsive behavioral pattern, and they are mostly inattentive. The symptoms of this disorder start in childhood; in fact, it can be visible as early as the age of three. But in usual cases, the symptoms can start any time before the child reaches the age of twelve. So, now, we are going to discuss the very common symptoms associated with ADHD –

Inattention

If you notice that your child is making silly mistakes in their school copies or they are not paying attention to even the smallest of things, then they are being inattentive. Some other instances of inattention are when your child does not respond the way they should even in cases when you are speaking to them directly. They might even show signs that they are not fully focused on games or even the simplest tasks during the day. Inattention can even be seen in forms where the child is easily distracted from the work that he/she is doing, and they even face trouble with organizational skills. You will understand that your child is being inattentive, if they try to dodge activities that require them to become focused, for example, homework. It can also be understood from situations where your child is losing important things that are required for assignments, or any other important matter.

Impulsivity and Hyperactivity

Does your child always prefer to stay in motion, or does he/she talk too much even when it is completely unnecessary? Then, these are symptoms of hyperactivity. You can say that they are showing impulsivity when they keep interrupting the questioner and blurt out answers when they are not supposed to. It is also when they are not able to wait for anything. Children with ADHD have this unavoidable need to interrupt others' games, conversations, and activities. They also show problems whenever they are asked to do some tasks in silence. They keep constantly fidgeting with their feet or hands or when asked to sit quietly for some time, they squirm in their seat. They even start climbing or running around especially when they are asked to sit in one place. This is also the reason why ADHD children face so many problems attending school.

Another common symptom is when your child is too much focused on his/her own needs that they completely ignore what others want. They face constant turmoil, and they are not able to put a rein on their emotions. In fact, they show anger outbursts amidst the most inappropriate situations. It is true that they might show their interest in a bunch of different things but when it comes to completing them before moving on to the next, they skip that part and leave that task incomplete.

Types

There is no one size fits all concept in the case of ADHD, mostly because the disorder takes a different shape for everyone. Although the symptoms are overall the same, the symptoms shown by any individual child might not be the same as another child. In this section, I am going to explain to you the different types of ADHD that are usually seen –

Primarily Hyperactive-Impulsive ADHD

This is seen in those kids whose main problem is that they want to continuously engage in some form of movement. They either struggle or keep fidgeting and don't want to stay in one place for a long time. They can never practice any form of self-control and often have the habit of blurting out things at the most unfortunate moments.

Primarily Inattentive ADHD

This is when children are not able to keep up with sustaining attention and, thus, end up making silly mistakes. Even if you provide them with a detailed set of instructions, they will not be able to follow them diligently and they are very bad at organizing stuff. No matter how small or insignificant the external stimulus is, kids suffering from this type of ADHD can get easily distracted.

Combination ADHD

Those kids whose symptoms do not entirely fall in any of the above-mentioned categories are the ones who have a little bit of both and are thus suffering from combination ADHD. This is also said to be the most common type among the three when it comes to children.

Diagnosis

Now that you know the symptoms, if you think that your child might be showing some of them, it is time that you talk to any general physician regarding it. If you are still concerned about whether you are taking the right step or not, you can even consult your child's teachers and see if they talk about the same symptoms displayed by the child in school as well. It is true that your general physician is not the person who will assess ADHD but going to them first is important. Some of the common questions that you might get asked while visiting the GP are as follows –

- ☆ What exact symptoms are you noticing in your child, and since when?
- ☆ When do the symptoms occur the most – when your child is in school or at home?
- ☆ Were there any recent traumatic or disturbing incidents in the life of your child?

- ☆ Do the symptoms make it difficult for your child to socialize with others?
- ☆ Do you have anyone in your family who has had ADHD?
- ☆ Are there any other symptoms not related to ADHD that seemed worth noticing to you?

After consulting the GP, the first thing that they would probably advise you to do is that keep your child under observation for a certain amount of time – usually, this time spans over ten weeks. This period will show whether your child goes through any improvement or not. You will also find out whether the symptoms worsen or remain the same.

In certain cases, you might also be advised for some education program or parent training that specifically focuses on ADHD. Now, there is something here that you need to understand – when you are being referred to attend parent training; it does not mean that you are bad at being a parent. It specifically aims at teaching you how you can handle your child better and improve their current condition. After this span of time, if you notice that the symptoms are not showing any signs of improvement, then it is time that you reach out for a formal assessment from a specialist.

If you are wondering what kind of specialist will you be referred to, well there are quite a few of them and you might be asked to visit any one of the following:

- ☆ If it is about children's health, a pediatrician is often recommended
- ☆ An adult or child psychiatrist depending on the age of the patient
- ☆ An occupational therapist, social worker, or learning disability specialist, all of whom should have proven expertise in ADHD cases.

The person you are being referred to usually varies with the location you are in and also the age of the actual patient. Whether or not your child is suffering from ADHD cannot be determined by any such single test. But a detailed assessment by someone expert in this matter definitely can throw light upon the matter. Some of the aspects of this assessment include –

- ☆ A series of interviews might be conducted not only with your child but you as well
- ☆ A physical examination of your child is done so that if there are any other physical conditions, then they can be brought to light
- ☆ Reports and interviews of some other people are also done, for example, teachers, family members, and partners.

But in order to diagnose a child or teenager with ADHD, there are certain criteria that need to be followed and I have explained them below –

- ☆ The symptoms had been started to show themselves before the child reached the age of 12.
- ☆ The symptoms have been visible and consistent for at least a period of six months.
- ☆ The symptoms should not be simply a part of any difficult phase that the child might be going through or any developmental disorder, and thus, they should not be accounted for any other underlying condition.
- ☆ The symptoms must be making it difficult for the child to lead a normal life both at academic and social levels.
- ☆ The symptoms should not only be showing themselves in one place but under two different settings, for example – at school and at home, so that the behavior shown by them is not a result of parental control or teacher's treatment.

Treatment

If you want the conditions of your child to improve and if you want him/her to lead a normal life without faltering at any of the day-to-day activities, then you have to opt for treatment. You can either go for therapy or medication, but the usual advice is that you should opt for a perfectly balanced combination of both. Any specialist can advise for the commencement of treatment.

Medication

Just for knowledge, I will now tell you about the five most types of medication for the treatment of ADHD, administered on a license but, I want to tell you to resort to these medicines only if recommended by your doctor and if strictly necessary.

Before we discuss these medications, you have to remember that there is no permanent cure for this disorder, and thus even if you use these medicines, your child is only going to get temporary relief from the symptoms. They will be able to practice new skills, learn new lessons, and have a calmer demeanor. There are certain types of medications that have to be administered after certain intervals and there are certain types that have to be taken daily.

No matter what type of medication is administered to your child, they will not be given any big doses at first for their own safety. In order to see the effect of the medications and to get your child used to them, small doses will be administered. With time, the doses can be increased on a gradual basis if such a thing is required. Moreover, you will also have to go for regular checkups to the specialist so that your child can be kept under regular monitoring. The specialist will also be able to tell whether the medications are working on your child or not. If there has been any side effect of the medications, don't hesitate to let your child's specialist know about it.

Now, let us move on to the common medications used in the treatment of ADHD.

- ☆ **Methylphenidate** – This is by far the most widely used and common medication administered to anyone suffering from ADHD. The best thing about it is that it can be offered to anyone, be it children, teenagers, or adults provided that the person it is being offered to is above the age of 5. This medicine is basically a stimulant and when administered, it acts on certain regions of the brain and helps in controlling your behavior and also enhanced attentive power. There are both modified-release and immediate-release tablets available for this medication. Some common side effects can be lack of sleep, an increase in heart rate and blood pressure, and stomach aches.
- ☆ **Dexamfetamine** – Just like methylphenidate, this medicine can be offered to anyone as long as that person is more than five years of age. It is taken as a tablet. In some cases, it might be administered twice a day, while in others, it might have to be taken once a day only. This medication can have some side

effects too like mood swings, a reduction in appetite, headaches, and dizziness among several others.

- ☆ **Lisdexamfetamine** – It is very similar to dexamfetamine, but it is administered to a person only when that person has been treated with methylphenidate for about six weeks, and yet there has been no improvement. This medication is available in the form of a capsule and some of its side effects include dizziness, aggression, a reduced appetite, and even diarrhea.
- ☆ **Atomoxetine** – This medication is not the same as the other three mentioned here. The amount of noradrenaline in your brain is increased by the intake of this medication. In case the above medications cannot be used for some reason, atomoxetine can be administered to anyone suffering from ADHD, provided they are above the age of 5. The side effects are the same as the above medications but in extreme cases, patients might even develop suicidal thoughts. That is why, if you find your child becoming depressed after using this medication, you need to talk to the doctor right away.
- ☆ **Guanfacine** – This medication has been known to reduce the level of blood pressure and improve attentive power. The medication is meant for kids above the age of 5, and it should not be

administered to adults. Some common side effects of this medication include dry mouth, abdominal pain, and tiredness.

Therapy

The other option is that you should take your child to therapy. There are different types of therapies that you can opt for and I have explained some of them in this section –

- ☆ **Behavior Therapy** – This type of therapy is not only for the child suffering from ADHD but also for his/her teachers and parents. A system is setup in which the child will be rewarded for displaying good behavior. Any type of behavior that you want your child to develop can be inculcated by this method, and when your child listens to you, you can give them a small reward.
- ☆ **Psychoeducation** – This will be a session where you along with your child. You will be encouraged to talk about ADHD and learn about its different side-effects. This type of therapy is usually helpful in making it easier for you to diagnose and understand the symptoms of ADHD.
- ☆ **Parent Training** – These programs are specifically meant for parents so that they learn about the new techniques in which they can improve their child's symptoms. These are usually group programs, and

you get to discuss with other parents going through the same phase as you.

- ☆ **Social Skills Training** – In these therapies, role-playing is used to teach the child how to socialize, and they also learn certain behaviors that they should do when they are in a public place.
- ☆ **CBT** – This is an acronym for Cognitive Behavioral Therapy. This therapy has gained quite a huge amount of popularity, especially because of its effectiveness when it comes to changing the way people think and perceive a situation. It can either be carried out as one-to-one sessions or even in a group.

Lookalikes

The behavioral issues that you are noticing in your child might not be the result of ADHD because there are certain conditions that look the same as ADHD but from within, they are something else. Let us have a look at some of these conditions –

- ☆ **Depression** –Depression is found in a lot of kids who are suffering from ADHD. It is said that one out of every seven kids suffering from ADHD also suffers from depression. In fact, when kids have ADHD, thcy are aulomatically stressed about it, and this stress can make matters worse. And what is even worse is that depression is also a side effect of the medications that are given in the case of ADHD. You will know that your child is probably depressed if you notice any changes in sleeping and eating habits.

- ☆ **Anxiety Disorders** –Among the kids having ADHD, 20% have anxiety problems mainly general anxiety, social anxiety, and also separation anxiety. In fact, when a child is already suffering from ADHD, he/she is more likely to become prone to anxiety than anyone else. And if that child is exposed to stimulants, then the conditions are bound to become worse.
- ☆ **Learning Disabilities** – It is said that learning disability is something that almost 50% of ADHD kids have, and in these cases too, children are disorganized and face difficulties in learning stuff. So, you should not get confused between the two. But there is one difference worth noting and that is – the intelligence of a child is affected in the case of ADHD but in learning disabilities, the intelligence doesn't reduce.
- ☆ **Bipolar Disorder** – Since the symptoms of ADHD and bipolar disorder are so overlapping that distinguishing between the two can become difficult at times.

#2

Debunking Common Myths About ADHD

Myths and misconceptions are present probably in every sphere of life, and ADHD is no different. But when these misconceptions form deeper roots in society, people actually start believing them, and then, they cannot distinguish what is true and what is false. That is why any misunderstanding regarding any disease can do lots of harm so it is of utmost importance that you remove any such myths by debunking them. Sometimes, it is these myths that cause a delay in treatment and leaves your children being misunderstood.

In this chapter, we are going to debunk the most common myths about ADHD.

ADHD Is Not Real

ADHD has been given the name of a medical condition time and again, but even then, some people think that it is not real and thus, it is not a medical condition. But you must know that the American Psychiatric Association and the National Institutes of Health both have declared the same – ADHD is a medical condition and it is very real. It is very common among children in the United States. As already discussed in the previous chapter, you saw that ADHD has a hereditary link. In fact, 1 out of every 4 kids having ADHD has a parent who has suffered from the same. There have been imaging studies that have proved the fact that those who have ADHD don't have the same level of brain development as compared to those who don't.

If you are someone who is experiencing ADHD or if your child is suffering from ADHD, know that it is very real, and your day-to-day life can be hugely affected because of it. Don't let society tell you any different. Moreover, I am going to give you tips and techniques for parenting a child with ADHD in the latter part of this book.

There are certain neurotransmitters in the brain which have some really important functions to perform but in the case of ADHD, they do not perform well, and thus, an imbalance is created. These neurotransmitters are – norepinephrine and dopamine. The regions of the brain that are gravely affected in this disorder are the prefrontal cortex which is where impulsivity originates and affects your judgment, limbic system which is the center of emotional control of your brain, the nucleus accumbens which is the region that makes you feel good, and locus ceruleous which can be called the arousal center.

Every Child Will Show the Same Symptoms

This is another myth that needs to be busted. Oftentimes, parents ignore their children's problems because they think that the symptoms shown by their child do not match the symptoms of their neighbor's kid who has already been diagnosed with ADHD. You have to remember that the symptom of this disorder will show itself in different ways in every individual. Every child faces certain difficulties, and their personal strengths also differ. That is why ADHD symptoms of hyperactivity, inattention, and impulsivity do not always reveal themselves in the same way. An example should make this clearer to you – some children might not be so talkative or fidgeting at all times but they might still have problems with personal organization or learning new things and thus, they might be diagnosed with ADHD.

ADHD Does Not Happen In Girls

ADHD affects everyone irrespective of their gender. But the claim that ADHD is not going to happen in girls is completely false. The reason why people believe in this myth is that girls don't always display behavioral issues like boys, and they are not always so hyperactive but that doesn't rule out the chance of ADHD. But what happens is that these girls who are actually suffering from ADHD but are not identified spend their entire lives without being diagnosed and so their condition keeps worsening. Some issues that get aggravated are their antisocial personality, anxiety, mood swings, and certain other comorbid disorders that they might have experienced in their childhood years.

That is why, I would say, whether you have a boy or girl, you should look out for any symptoms equally. You don't want your girl to be left untreated just because she had a quiet attitude. She might be showing other symptoms of ADHD and when you identify those symptoms, you have to give them all the support they need.

ADHD Happens When Kids Are Lazy

This is just a way of demeaning the problem because ADHD is not caused by laziness or lack of motivation. It is a real medical issue and has to be addressed in that manner. When your kids are suffering from ADHD, it is not that they are not trying to pay attention to things. They are actually trying their best, but they can't really do so. If you are asking your child to focus more and being angry at them because they are not trying, it is somewhat similar to being angry on someone for not being able to see when in reality, they are blind.

The attitude of your child is not a factor affecting the attentive power of your child. It is because of physical differences in their brain, and they cannot see or do things like other kids. You cannot expect them to behave or perform like other kids when they are not built in the same way.

In fact, people who don't understand ADHD often blame the kids for not being productive or focused, but that makes the child feel guilty and worsen his/her symptoms. When a child has ADHD, you have to set a lot of reminders to make them do a task but that does not mean they are lazy; it simply means that they do not have the mental structure required to put in so much effort. Sometimes playing a simple game of building blocks can become mentally exhausting for a kid suffering from ADHD and that is why you should not be judging them for staying behind others.

Kids With ADHD Will Eventually Grow Out of Their Symptoms

ADHD doesn't really ever go away. If some people don't show the symptoms anymore, it is because they have learned to cope with it over time. In fact, you can call ADHD a lifelong disorder. It has been estimated that if a person shows symptoms in childhood, then 60% of all those people are going to carry the disorder into their adulthood. And the other 40% of the patients have learned how to turn their disorder in a positive direction and control it effectively. ADHD no longer can control their emotions and actions and they have finally been able to do that over the course of the years. And this can be successful for your child too only if you take him/her to therapy or introduce them to medication and intervene in the problem at an early stage of life.

According to the estimates, about 6% of the adults in the U.S are still coping with the symptoms of ADHD, and among them, one out of every four people actually opt for therapy in order to get support. But these figures are not at all healthy because ADHD has to be addressed and you cannot simply let it be because, with time, it can lead to substance issues, anxiety, and co-morbid depression. They even face a lot of struggles when it comes to their relationship and career.

It Is Bad Parenting That Causes ADHD

It has often been noticed that the parents of those suffering from ADHD often start feeling that maybe it was their fault that their child started showing symptoms of ADHD. They feel guilty and keep wishing what if they did things differently? But you have to remember that this is only a myth – ADHD is not a result of poor parenting because it has scientific reasons behind its origin.

When the child is suffering from ADHD, they are constantly punishing themselves for the symptoms they show, and that is why they display impulsivity, hyperactivity, and restlessness. All of these symptoms can actually be very harmful to you in the long run. And in certain cases, parents do not recognize these signs as symptoms of ADHD and think that their child is only ill-mannered. In fact, outsiders often judge parents of kids with ADHD to be not controlling and not knowing to parent and that, in turn, can affect the mental health of the parent.

People With ADHD Lose Their Ability to Focus

This myth can be a confusing one, and that is why debunking it becomes all the more important. You have already read in the previous chapter and probably heard it several times that when someone is suffering from ADHD, one of the main things that they struggle with is focusing. But that is not the case every time. Sometimes, children with ADHD become so much focused on a certain issue that it is called hyperfocus.

There are certain ADHD affected students who will never be able to understand anything in the game that they are playing or be able to decipher things that are being taught in the class. But there are also some kids who tend to hyperfocus. Things can easily go out of hand at times. This is because anyone who is into hyper-focusing, they might not notice the dangers present right in front of them because they are too focused on something else.

ADHD Medications Can Lead to Substance Abuse

I don't know what leads to believing in this myth, but this is not at all true. In fact, what happens is that when you are giving your ADHD child the right medications for their problem, they are most likely not going to turn to any type of recreational drugs to solve their problems or feel better. But it is when the child is not receiving the treatment he/she should receive that they turn to other things to solve their problems. Some might even try to self-medicate with alcohol just because they are not getting the right treatment.

It Is a Type of Learning Disability

You have to know that ADHD is not a learning disability at all. I have mentioned this time and again and I am going to say this again – it is a medical condition, and it has to be treated like one. It is true that the symptoms seen in the case of ADHD can definitely get in the way of your learning but these are symptoms of ADHD and not a separate learning disability. Also, some kids show both ADHD and learning disability and that is also one of the reasons why this myth is believed in so much.

Now that you know the myths about ADHD, I hope you are going to rectify others too when they believe in some myth like this. The reason for these myths is because you cannot really see

ADHD visually. It is a neurobiological disorder and it is there but people find it easier to judge it just because they cannot see it. But you have to understand that at times, ADHD patients are only hanging by a thread, and judging them might do them irreparable harm.

#3

5 Reinforcements for ADHD

In this chapter, we are going to talk about the five most important reinforcements that can increase the symptoms of ADHD. These children are always in need of support, and they want to depend on another person and when they can get the complete attention of their caregivers, it soothes them and makes them feel well. When the ADHD children are growing, their parents and everyone around them expect them to take care of themselves and abide by certain rules. Hurling ADHD children with all sorts of restrictions aren't going to solve the problem

You simply have to understand what actions can actually benefit your ADHD child and improve their behavior and what actions can make their situation worse. And when you know these and you know the reinforcements of the negative effects of ADHD, you can actually help in reducing those things. The five main reinforcements have been discussed in this chapter,which sometimes can work in unison with other behaviors to make your child's symptoms worse.

Attention

Now the acronym ADHD stands for Attention Deficit Hyperactivity and so the first reinforcement that we are going to talk about is attention. You will notice that whenever you are with your child, and you start talking to someone else rather affectionately, your child is going to start behaving in a boisterous way. This is mostly because children suffering from ADHD often get threatened and nervous whenever they see their parents sharing some affectionate relationships with others. Some common actions depicting this include your child making noises or doing something as soon as you shift your attention from here to someone else. They might even keep targeting things that are off their limits. When your child performs such actions, it is because they really want to bring to your notice what they have been up to. Sometimes you do not even have to speak to someone but a simple facial expression is enough to trigger this kind of activity.

It is true that a child automatically becomes too self-centered when he/she starts showing symptoms of ADHD. In fact, if your child is currently acting insane, hyperactive, busy, distracting, or annoying, you will find it next to impossible to go away from her or make her sit at one place while you will complete your chores. One thing that helps is by flopping your lap when your child is sitting and then talking to someone.

At home or at school, a child can garner a lot of attention when they are performing certain off-task activities. If you find that your child is not able to follow the instructions gives to them and are fiddling all the time, then everyone becomes concerned even at school. That is when the teachers try to reach out to your child so that she can comply with the instructions. This, in turn, makes your child that they hold certain importance here, and other people are really concerned about her. This leads to an opportunity when you can motivate the child and support him/her. In fact, in certain cases, the child might also like it when you plead them to give an answer to a question or if you repeat their name frequently. In this way, they feel important. In fact, because of the inattentive nature of ADHD children, they are often made to sit beside the instructor or the teacher in public gatherings and this special attention makes them feel good and suppresses their symptoms too.

You have to remember and remind yourself that not every child is the same, and so, there are some kids suffering from ADHD who need a little bit of more support and attention as compared to others. When you are in public spaces and waiting rooms, your child can easily get out of control and garner an audience of their own. They might behave loudly and not listen to what you are trying to say. For example, let us say that you are trying to read a book while waiting for the train while your child is sitting with you. They might try to distract you not because they are mean but because they want to spend more time with you. They might even do something amusing to make you feel impressed. But you cannot really impose any restrictions on your child in a public space because everyone keeps staring.

When your child makes such tantrums to get attention, there is no need to worry that maybe he/she doesn't get enough tantrums. It is only because they don't really have friends and so they depend entirely on you. In fact, they might even have to face multiple transgressions and jokes when they go out.

Accommodation

In usual cases, a child refrains from showing a vigorous ADHD behavior as long as you are saying 'yes' to them. It is normal for the loved ones of the child to provide him/her with comfort and support the moment the child starts to create problems or whine. These things happen often when your child is showing symptoms of anxiety, is being too self-critical, is displaying rage, or is overreacting. Whenever a child in the family is diagnosed with ADHD, adults try to offer all their support to the child and instantly, lower all their expectations too.

Socially accommodating a child can also create a lot of problems. For example, if your child is acting out and asking you to bring something to them so that their discomfort can be soothed, you go and bring that thing for him/her and in fact, bring it in more quantities so that your child does not have to face any discomfort. So, your child understands that whenever they display bad behavior, they are going to get more stuff. ADHD symptoms tend to flare up when you do more for your child and put a lot of effort.

Let me give you another very common example, and it will be cleared for you to understand. When your child is not paying attention to things, whether it is at home or at school, they might ask you to explain that matter to them because they were not attentive. In this way, they keep relying on you, and in the end, they do not learn how to take care of their own self or their own needs. And if you cannot get your child come out of this toxic behavior and cycle of ADHD, they are not going to see progress in any sphere of life. And teachers in the school are not always trying to help every individual speed and bring them up to speed. So, you have to inculcate values of self-care in your child.

In fact, in certain cases, the child starts to correlate rescue with love. This is because whenever they are in some sort of dangerous circumstance or difficult place in life, you will try your best to help them out and remove them from such a situation. But that act makes an ADHD child feel that if they put themselves in dangerous situations, then they are going to get all the love from you and thus be valuable.

When a child is accommodated from time to time, you will often find that they keep bombarding you with questions that they either know the answer to or know how to solve on their own. Do you know why? This is mainly because parents often leave behind everything to simply answer the questions of their children, and ADHD children prefer this. They want you to do this. And that is why they might even play stupid or dumb when in reality, they are not. This type of behavior often raises assistance from parents because they know that they cannot enforce any conditions on the child or make the child feel accountable. It is your duty to help your child overcome his/her trials and whenever they are being ineffective at something, you are there to help him/her out. Your child might also complain about you not telling them everything or not interfering in certain things and the reason you are not doing it because your child is not qualified for those things. This can make the symptoms worse.

An attitude of self-gratification in a very toxic form develops when you are attending to every worry and every need of your child even at the expense of your own well-being. In such cases, children with ADHD are being pampered at every step of the way and so they never really learn what others desire or need. If you accommodate your ADHD child too much and give them easements at every turn so that they can achieve their goals, it will backlash later on when they are not able to do things because of the lack of someone to help them out.

So, from all the above explanations and examples, it must have become clear to you that you cannot really fight the symptoms of ADHD if you keep accommodating your child more than it is required. But now we are going to discuss the several reasons behind this over-accommodating habit of parents –

- ☆ Although there are different reasons for a parent accommodating his/her child too much, the most common one is that they feel that if they do not do something, their child might be in danger. So, ADHD parents always try to take the safe route because they do not want their child to get hurt in any way. They know the potential risks involved, and so they won't ever wish it on their kids.
- ☆ Another reason is that when shame gets in the way of things, parents compromise even more easily. An example should make this clearer. Let us say a couple has gone through a divorce, and then the single mother finds out that the child is suffering from ADHD. Then she is in a lot of shame and guilt and starts blaming herself because she thinks ADHD happened due to negligence on her part. And this leads to her over-accommodating the child in every aspect of life. She also

starts blaming herself for having worked too many hours outside and not being able to be there for her child. But as I have already debunked that myth, I am not going into the details. Although I would definitely want to remind you that ADHD is not a result of bad parenting – it has a medical reason behind it.

- ☆ Another common reason for over-accommodating a child is because the parents had faced a lot of poverty while growing up, and now when they have a child of their own, they do not want the child to go through a similar phase. So, they take care of the situation by providing the child with everything and sometimes – in a way that is more than necessary.
- ☆ The next reason that we are going to discuss is trauma. Parents try to solve every single problem that the child might be facing after trauma so that he/she does not have to deal with any kind of threat themselves, but in the process of doing that, the parents end up over-accommodating the child.
- ☆ And then there are parents who give in to over-accommodation because they simply do not have enough time in their hands which they can give to the child and help him/her to learn something on their own. They might be busy because of their work

schedule or even because they have to deal with a lot of family burdens.

So, no matter what your or cause of over-accommodation is, it is not going to help the child in any way, and in fact, it can hamper with their self-management skills. As a parent, it is very natural for you to think that you are going to make your child's life easy, but you also have to realize that learning to do things by yourself is a skill that every child needs in order to survive. You will not be there at all times to look after your child even if he/she is suffering from ADHD and then if the child is not prepared to look after their own, then they will feel abandoned. Yes, when you are helping your child out, you are developing a special bond with them but at the same time, you are also pushing them in a situation where they won't be able to do the simplest things in life if you do not provide them feedback.

As parents, you will feel at peace when you know that your child is safe with you, but at the same time, you have to prepare them for the time when you'll not be there and so they have to be self-reliant.

Suppose your child is doing some project, and you are making your best effort to make things simplified for him/her, then you are actually not helping your child. The kids have to learn to exert themselves and when you do the tasks for them, they love to hide behind that and they never end up doing anything by themselves. If you keep reminding them of the things they have to take or in fact, take their things yourself so that the child does not forget them, they will never learn to remember things or recall them if you are not there. Yes, when you help your child even with the easiest tasks, it saves a lot of time and energy and in fact, simplifies certain situations but the fact is – you are not preparing them for their own future and you are allowing the ADHD symptoms to sustain themselves.

Avoidance

When faced with adversity, one of the most common ways to deal with problems is avoidance. When you are giving in to avoidance, it can actually keep the inability to focus and distractibility going on for an indefinite period of time.

The moment a child has been found out to have ADHD, everyone surrounding the child, including the parents, give up on understanding anything that is going on with the child – be it their inability to adapt or cooperate. The only thing they deduce from the entire situation is that there is no use talking to the child because the ADHD symptoms are going to prevent him/her from paying attention to the conversation. They simply take it for granted that the child is not going to learn anything ever, no matter how hard they try, and that is why they don't try at all.

In case the child does not respond to something the way he/she should and continues to do what he/she is doing, then the parents often take it that it is because of the ADHD child's hyper-focusing attitude that is stopping them from listening to the parents. Even if there is a lack of courtesy in the child, everyone will keep saying that it is because of the ADHD symptoms that all of this is happening.

But all of these responses are nothing but distractive comments. Sometimes they can benefit your child because they can finally move on with whatever they want to do because people no longer judge their actions. But when the child realizes that no one really wants to hear what he/she has to say, they start doing the same and don't listen to what anyone else has to say to them. And that is why the child completely changes topics even when elders are trying to discuss something important, or they cow away from acknowledging stuff and instead, start daydreaming.

It is because of this distractibility that the child gets to go away from all kinds of punishment, assessment, and restrictions. They become too absorbed in whatever they are doing and stop responding to any outside things. If you start nagging at things, even then your child will not listen to you and instead become lethargic.

From the outside, you might feel that your child is showing distracted attitude, incapability of almost anything, and an unfocused nature, but usually what happens is that the child is trying to avoid all those things that disrupt him/her. This is because if they start showing those things, then others will make them feel that they are a source of disappointment and they don't want to feel that way. So, instead, they choose not to hear anything negative about themselves. But if others can make the child feel safe and be appreciative of whatever qualities they have, then the child will stop being so immersive and open up.

Sometimes elders brush aside a lot of things calling them impulsive attitude, but if you look deep down, then you will realize that they are nothing but avoidance. For example, if the child starts being a rebel all of a sudden by doing something reckless or rash, you might call her impulsive but the child might be just trying to avoid something and walk away from the situation. And in engaging in an impetuous activity, the child not only distracts others but also their own self.

Acquisition

Sometimes there are certain acts of the ADHD kids that allow them easy and fast access to things they want. If there is some sudden reckless behavior and the child wants something from the parent, the parent is highly likely to give that item to the child. It is because of the impulsive actions of a child suffering from ADHD that you do not know what they are going to do next. They might harass in inappropriate ways or they might even pick on others, and this is also what gives them the things they want because parents don't want the behavior to continue. At times, the child might even blurt out certain words or things about someone that they were not supposed to say but they do so anyway. These are what impulsive actions look like.

The child actually enjoys all the things he/she gets because of the behavior, but in most cases, it also brings trouble down the line. But when the problems become too much in the future, others have to interfere to smooth things out. But what you, as a parent, should keep an eye on is how many types the kid's rashness is making you fall in trouble and someone else has to step in to save the situation.

Antagonism

The last reinforcement that we are going to discuss is antagonism. When a child is upset, there might be times when they want to strike back. Usually, the kids suffering from ADHD are subtle, and the most they will do is flip some household objects or do something annoying on purpose. But if you show frustration and exasperation, your child will gradually learn how to make you feel annoyed. But the most common question that almost every parent has is why does the child antagonize in the first place? Well, this is mostly because of some type of relationship issues. If you want your child to come out of the cycle of conflict, then you have to figure out a way to deal with the antagonism.

A child suffering from ADHD is not always aware of the exact reason that is bothering them. Even when the child is showing anger at you, it might not be you who he/she is angry but something completely different which you might not know about. A parent is a safe space for a child, and that is why that is the first place where they take out their anger. At other times, the antagonism happens because the parent was not attentive enough or did not keep up with a request that the child made.

If you are trying to figure out why your child was behaving antagonistically, then I must tell you that it is not going to be as easy as you think. It is not so simple to untangle relationships because they are highly complex. There might be some old incidents that are triggering the antagonistic attitude in your child.

With all this fighting between you and your child, you might be wondering whether it is doing you any kind of benefit at all. Well, I must say that what benefits is the making up after the fight. It strengthens the bond. Yes, when the fight happened, and you overreacted, you might be feeling bad for it or you might be feeling that what you did was not right but now when you are trying to make up for it, you will feel good because, without the fight, that moment would not have happened. Most ADHD kids have the same trait and that is they prefer whenever they are ones dominating. On some days, you will find that your child is not willing to forgive you at once and they require some added effort of pleading but then they will eventually forgive you.

But it is also important that you keep an eye out for the triggers that make your child behave in that manner. It can be anything – an incident that happened in school, something you said unknowingly, or anything that happened in the past. The most common causes of these ADHD symptoms are depleted parents, an inferiority complex, and incompetence insinuations.

Learning Self-Care

One of the very first steps of dealing with ADHD is to teach your child how they can care for themselves. As parents, you will obviously be taking care of your child, but when your child knows how to take care of themselves, there is nothing better than that because slowly, they will learn how to be self-reliant. And with that, children suffering from ADHD also learn how they can follow through and stay on track.

It is important that you teach your child not to depend on your verbal instructions alone but to do things by themselves. This will help them gain autonomy, but simultaneously, they also need to indulge in some self-care. You also have to try and foster enthusiasm about the things that they love in life. One very common example is to make your child learn how they can listen to an alarm clock to wake up and not depend only on the voice of their mother. But you also have to show your faith and your love in your children and show them that they are actually worth believing in. No matter what happens, you cannot give up on the child. Whether it is about pouring their own juice in the glass or applying toothpaste on the toothbrush, every small task can be accomplished if they have the right support.

The accountability background and scale of your child might not be what it should be for a child of his/her age, but that is okay. It is usually said that an ADHD child is behind others in day-to-day activities by as much as 30% and their self-management skills take the hit. So, if you want to teach your child how to engage in active self-care, here are some strategies that you should follow –

Stress On the Advantages

I know when I am talking about self-care, you probably might be conjuring up some luxurious thoughts but that is not what self-care is all about. It can be practiced in your own way. It can be a set of practical actions made, especially for the well-being of your ADHD child.

If you want to give your child the best self-care you have to urge then to figure out what they really want. When ADHD children are not permitted to look after themselves or engage in self-care, they become even more exhausted, depressed, emotionally depleted, or even angry. When you teach your child how to put him or her on the top of their priority list, they will stop feeling overwhelmed and undeserving. Yes, at times, your teenage child might feel that they will start looking after themselves once everything becomes okay but that can become a far-fetched dream. You need to put yourself first now and teach your kids to do the same.

At first, if you ask your child to think about self-care, they might feel uncomfortable. So, don't rush it. Take it one day at a time and teach them small actions, all of which will go into making themselves feel better.

But there are cases when the children actually move farther away from their parents when they are asked to become self-sustainable. This is because children with ADHD always need someone by them, and when you ask them to start learning to do their own things, they fear that you are going to abandon them. They have this risk of rejection in their heads that can be toxic and prevents them from adopting a self-sustaining lifestyle.

In case you notice these things in your child as well, it is time that you take a different approach and start asking some questions to your child like – "Do you think I am going to love you any less if you started to take care of yourself?" You have to make your child realize that you want them to grow more in life, and that is why you are urging them to take care of themselves.

You have to make them understand the different advantages of self-reliance. Give them some examples like – when they become self-reliant, they can go visit many places, and they can complete tasks even when someone is not present to help them out. The main idea is that you have to make the child realize there is more good to being self-reliant than the bad. You have to be very careful with the tone of voice and word usage because an ADHD child can get affected very easily. After everything you say, see how your child is reacting – whether it is positive or negative. If it's positive, then you will know that you are doing it the right way. You can also keep a note of your child's willingness to become self-reliant and the self-growth that he/she is showing every day so that you can track how far you have come with teaching them self-care.

Teach Them to Follow Through On Commitments

As discussed in the previous chapter, if you help your kids to do even the smallest tasks, then you are actually saving time and also making them feel they are important and valuable, but are you helping them for their future? ADHD kids have difficulty following through anything, be it commitments or instructions. So, here are some ways in which you can teach the concept of commitment to your ADHD child without flaring up the symptoms –

Work On Organizational Skills

One of the biggest challenges that every ADHD kid's parent faces is teaching their child how to follow through. The genuine reason behind this is the lack of organizational skills in ADHD children, and that is also why they keep forgetting all the obligations they had. But there are also certain cases in which the parents unknowingly promote their kids to use ADHD as an excuse to avoid almost everything in life. Just because a child has ADHD doesn't mean that they do not have what it needs to be productive. They can get up in the morning and follow a routine just like you and me. You simply have to teach them all of it in the right way.

One such strategy is by taking the help of a planner to help your ADHD child brush up on his/her organizational skills. When you teach them how a planner is used, you should also show them how they can map out their tasks in it. You have to teach them to make their own routine. For example, let us consider that your child has a number of assignments to submit at school in the upcoming weeks. Then you have to tell to make the entries accordingly in the planner so that they can keep track of the things they need to get done within a particular date.

But writing down all these to-do lists and deadlines is not all that they should do. There is a lot more work involved. Once the deadlines have been prepared, it will be your duty as a parent to teach your child how to use the planner in the first place. You have to teach them how to break a single assignment into different parts and then focus on one part at a time and treat these small parts as stepping stones to their ultimate goal. Similarly, if any exams are coming up in school, you have to teach your child how they can come up with a study plan to complete everything on time before the exams. Every day in the planner needs to have a goal no matter how big or small it is. Then, you also have to teach them to figure out their own strategies to fulfill their goal. In this way, slowly yet steadily, the child will become fully invested in their studies.

Practice Color-Coding

The next strategy that you can use to help your ADHD child work on his/her organizational skills is color-coding. It's true that ADHD children are definitely going to face some academic challenges, but that doesn't give them any excuse for giving up on stuff. Color coding is one such strategy that has always helped others suffering from ADHD to learn things quickly. You can separate the different subjects in your planner in different colors. This will help you understand stuff with just a single glance at your planner.

One way of implementing color coding is as follows – suppose your child has Math homework, and you have assigned the color yellow to math. Then, make sure they put some yellow labels where they are doing the homework and also make them wear a yellow bracelet to school so that they don't forget that they had math homework and that they have completed it. The bracelet helps a lot because it serves to be a visual reminder of the homework. Once the assignment is checked by the teacher, the child can then take the bracelet off and put it in their bag.

If you want to take things a bit further, then make folders for each subject and label then in a certain color. Organizational skills are made quite strong with color coding, and your child will be able to follow through easily.

Pets Can Be Implemented to Teach Being Responsible

When a child is suffering from ADHD, pets can do wonders for them. Pets can help to bring a sense of routine and responsibility for the child. This is because pets bring in a burst of positivity at once. You can get your child anything they want – be it a cat, dog, or even a rabbit. Whatever the pet is, you have to give your child the responsibility of feeding the pet and take them out for walks if applicable. Your child will try their best to maintain the responsibility because they love the pet and taking care of them gives them back an equal amount of love.

Moreover, getting a pet like a dog or a cat is even better because even if your child forgets to feed them once, the pet will keep reminding them some way or the other about feeding. Animals have their own ways of making things understand. Also, when you gift your ADHD child with a pet, it will make them feel they are responsible. Sometimes, a little amount of motivation or push is all a student needs to get going.

Encourage Good Hygiene

Children who are presently suffering from ADHD face difficulties in doing even the simplest things in life, and that also includes maintaining proper hygiene. From the outside, it might feel that your child is not brushing teeth or taking a shower daily but on the inside, they are feeling a lot of things. Being a parent to an ADHD child is not easy but you have to take it one day at a time and take the baby steps necessary for teaching your child how to take care of their personal hygiene. Kids who have ADHD usually get stuck in one particular thought, moment, or activity and it takes them a lot of time to get done with something.

You might be telling your child a thousand times to shower or to brush their teeth, and yet they keep forgetting because this is not how you should inculcate good personal hygiene values. If you are the person who is constantly telling them what to do and what not to do, then there will be a point of time where they will not be able to function until and unless you are present with them. Moreover, when you keep nagging with the same things, some children can hate it because it acts as a constant reminder that you doubt their abilities.

When you agonize too much about the poor hygiene of your child, they might like that attention and keep doing intentionally so that you give all your attention to them.

One of the factors that aids in the resistance shown by ADHD kids towards personal hygiene are the use of negative words in the case of parents. Any form of negativity can work against the well-being of your ADHD child. When you constantly keep checking on your child to make sure they have brushed their teeth or washed their hands will make them see these usual activities in a negative light as if they are some unpleasant activities. Your word usage should be complimenting the child, and they should be encouraging him/her to maintain proper hygiene. They should not display even a shred of doubt on their abilities.

If you want your child to brush teeth regularly, you can make a subtle recommendation that dentists always advise you to brush teeth on a regular basis; otherwise, you are going get cavities. You should not ask them to do anything. Sometimes remarks like these are enough to make an ADHD child do a task. Also, you can teach your child how to brush or floss in the correct manner. This will encourage them to do it correctly as well. You should also tell your child how great they look when they have brushed their teeth because of a whiter smile.

Some parents keep aiming for perfection even if their child is doing an activity. Don't do that. Let your child brush his/her teeth. Take it one step at a time. If you keep pestering on the fact that the brushing was not right, they might not brush at all. So, don't stress on being perfect with everything.

Help Them to Develop Routines

There is no perfect or imperfect way to raise a child who is suffering from ADHD. But one thing that is very important when it comes to parenting is that you should instill a structured environment for your child, and they should be introduced to the concept of routines. The first question that you are probably having is how a structure is going to help your child. We are going to discuss all of them in this section.

Why Is Routine Important?

Whenever we are having a discussion about the right way to bring up a child with ADHD, you will often come across the term structure. Do you know what it refers to? It is an environment that is more predictable and organized. In order to bring structure to your child's life, you have to create a schedule for them and make routines for their day-to-day life. Your child should clearly understand the consequences, expectations, and rules so that their environment is predictable. This, in turn, helps them in feeling secure. The ability to regulate themselves is something that

ADHD kids do not possess. They have so many distractions, and staying concentrated on any one particular thing becomes next to impossible for them.

Self-control is a very big issue for kids suffering from ADHD, and we are going to discuss more of it in the next chapter but in this chapter, we are going to talk about routines, why they are important, and how you can set them. With the presence of a routine, completing simple tasks will no longer seem like a burden to the child. They will learn how to set some time out for things like taking a shower, brushing their teeth, or doing their homework. In simpler terms, with these routines, you will be able to teach some good habits to your kids.

How to Develop a Routine?

The most confusing thing about all of this is how you are going to develop the routine for your kids. If you are at such crossroads too, then don't worry because I have included some important points as to how this can be done.

- ☆ The first thing that you should do is ensure that your instructions are very clear and to the point. If you want your child to clean their room, don't give them any instruction that says – 'Clean your room.' Instead, you have to be specific about what you want them to do; for example, you can ask them to 'put the books on the shelf and the toys in the cupboard.' This is what a specific instruction looks like. ADHD children have to be told exactly what you are expecting and only then they can work.

- ☆ It is also important for you to assign those tasks to your child that you know he will be able to do on his own. When they get success in one of the tasks, it promotes them even more to do other things; that is, they start developing confidence. On the other hand, if you give them some tasks that they are not able to do on their own, it will only demotivate them even more. The entire aim of developing a routine is to encourage your child to complete his/her tasks on their own.
- ☆ Always incorporate some kind of physical activity in their routines. This is very important if you want your child to remain mentally and physically fit. For kids suffering from ADHD, physical activity can be quite stimulating and is also advised by doctors and specialists. In case there is bad weather, you should schedule any physical activity inside the house.
- ☆ You should write down the routines for your child. The tasks cannot be clumped together. You have to write them down in a sequence. Each sequence should have anywhere between two to five tasks; otherwise, your child is going to become

confused. You can post this routine at a place where it will easily be noticed by your child. A written set of instructions are always better for ADHD children because verbal instructions can be forgotten very easily. In case your child has to complete a larger task, you have to break that big task into small steps for him/her. This will ensure that your child stays on track.

- ☆ Another great way of ensuring that this routine and schedule system works for your child is to establish a set of rules for receiving rewards. Whenever your child completes some tasks as they were asked to do, you should set a particular reward that they will be given.
- ☆ Don't expect your child to show huge improvements right away. You have to give them a sufficient amount of time. They literally have to give up their old habits and form new ones, and that does not happen overnight. So, you have to expect gradual improvement and not a sudden one.
- ☆ Sometimes, the efforts of your child might not always yield any results, but that is fine. You have to acknowledge the fact that your child is at least trying to be better. The reward for good behavior should be more frequent than the times you punish them for something bad.

- ☆ Lastly, don't cram up their routine too much. You have to keep some free time for your kids to do what they please. Everyone needs their own downtime and so scheduling some free time is also important.

How Does a Typical Routine Look Like?

In order to give you a better idea about the entire process, I have listed what a typical routine for an ADHD child should look like. The example is just for reference and that the routine that you are making for your child does not have to necessarily match this one.

Morning Routine –

- ☆ The first thing to ensure in your kid's morning routine is that they should have a fixed time of waking up. You can either wake them up personally with your touch, or you can also make them get used to an alarm clock.
- ☆ Then, you have to make a checklist of your kid's morning hygiene, which typically includes brushing teeth, making the bed, taking a shower, and changing into fresh clothes. In case your child has any fixed medications to take during the day, you can add take meds to the list.

- ☆ Note down the time for breakfast and give them options too. Ensure that you are not mentioning too many artificial or packaged food products.
- ☆ Then, make a section any time during the morning where your child has to take care of the pet. This can include cleaning their cage, giving them food and water, or taking them out for a walk.
- ☆ After that comes the section of morning study or chores. If they have school on any particular day then this time is going to be blocked by school activities, but in case they do not have school, you can pick some very specific tasks for them like homework, or you can have a weekly chore chart for them which can make things even easier. But for every chore that you write, make sure you break the time gaps accordingly.

After-School Routine –

- ☆ If your child had school, then they need to have a routine for things they have to do after returning from school. And the first thing to include is snack time. You should give some healthy options to them and keep those snacks ready.
- ☆ Like I mentioned before, physical activity is important, and so you should fix a time for your child in the late afternoon when they can play outside with their ball or any

other particular activity that they like to do.

- ☆ Then, keep time for napping, and the time span will vary with their age.
- ☆ In the evening, you have to jot down exactly what chores you want your child to do. If they have homework, then keep a specific time for that.
- ☆ Then, once they have done the chores, fix a time for watching television. But remember, excessive television is not a good idea, and so, you should be allowing them to watch TV only for a fixed duration of time.
- ☆ Before dinner, you can ask your child to clean up their room, and here too, you have to be very specific about what you want them to do exactly.

Dinner Routine –

- ☆ If your child if of age, then you can ask them to help you in making dinner. And if you want that, then you can make a checklist for them related to the dinner.
- ☆ Keep some time after dinner, during which you can plan some relaxation activities for them. As you might now, when childs have ADHD, they find it troublesome to calm their minds down or settle down. Activities that do not require

a lot of energy like board games can be a good thing to engage in post-dinner.

Bedtime Routine –

- ☆ Lastly, at the end of the day, you have to prepare a very detailed bedtime routine. Start by listing things like brushing your teeth, wash your face, put on your pajamas, and place your used clothes in the laundry basket.
- ☆ Then, if they have school the next day, you can ask them to prepare their school bag and also keep the clothes for the next day in the appropriate place.
- ☆ Sometimes ADHD children are not able to fall asleep quickly because of their restless nature and so, you can either put on some relaxing music, or you can read to them. You can also give them a mini-massage of about fifteen minutes where you will not be using any firm pressure but simply make them feel relaxed.
- ☆ The time for going to bed has to be kept the same for ADHD children otherwise, they can face troubles sleeping. Also, if they have to take any medications before sleeping, make sure you include that in the routine as well.

Assist Them Overcome Difficulties With Dressing Up

The entire act of putting on clothing can become really difficult for an ADHD child, but you can make it better for them by following some simple steps. Some of them have problems with the type of fabrics that the clothes have or some of them might forget the sequence in which they should put on their clothes. The problems vary from one child to another.

- ☆ The first thing that you have to do is calm your child done. If your child takes a shower in the morning, you have to first dry them off completely using a towel that is heavily textured. It has been noticed that the use of textured towels can calm down the brains of ADHD children, and then dressing them becomes easier. This gives them tactile stimulation.
- ☆ Some ADHD kids have shown symptoms of feeling more secure when they wore underwear that is tight-fitting. In that case, you can go for underwear that is snug-fitted like performance apparel. But make sure the fabrics are of high-quality and breathable so that your child can wear the clothes throughout the day and yet now feel too sweaty or uncomfortable.
- ☆ You will often find ADHD kids complaining about how their clothes are feeling itchy, but parents sometimes tend

to overlook such things and don't believe them. You should not do this. If they say that the clothing is uncomfortable, believe them. Try to buy clothes only in those fabrics that your child seems to love the most. Make sure the clothes do not have any tags or anything else that might cause irritation.

- ☆ The clothing should be simple, and that is why pants having waistbands that can simply be pulled up are advised over pants that have zippers and buttons. You can give your child dressing lessons on how they can button their shirts or how they can tie their laces on the weekends.
- ☆ Children with ADHD often get frustrated when they have to put on too complex shoes and socks. Stick to socks that are short and shoes that have Velcro straps in place of shoes that have laces.
- ☆ Lastly, you have to provide your child with all the support you can, and so, you have to break down the entire process of dressing up into small steps for your child to understand it properly. Don't dress them up fully. You can start the process and then let them finish by following the instructions. All of these small achievements are going to boost your child's confidence and make the rest of the day easier for them.
- ☆ Another thing to keep in mind is that your child's clothing closet should not be untidy

or overflowing. This will make them confused as to what they should wear or where a particular shirt or pant is. You should keep their clothes categorized. Never hang the clothes in places where your child will have difficulty to reach. If there are clothes in the closet that are not for this season, you can keep those clothes on the top shelf so as to prevent any confusion in your child.

☆ Lastly, don't mock your child for any wardrobe mismatches. If an ADHD child is taking an initiative to dress themselves up, you have to support their enthusiasm instead of crushing it. The dressing sense will come with age and time. You have to be patient and teach them all about color coordination sometime later. Also, avoid any kind of distractions when your child is getting ready. Some parents keep the TV on and this is very wrong in the case of ADHD children. This will divert their mind. You have to allow them to concentrate fully on the dress and so you should also ask other family members not to distract the child while he/she is dressing.

A Gift For You

Yes, you got it right! I have a gift for you who read this book. If you sign up at this link https://forms.gle/eLjRcnNRAm6mZaaDA I'll send you some important tools to realize your token economy or your daily routine.

Learning Self-Control

It is very common for ADHD kids not to think properly before they act out. And this is also the reason why they fall into trouble so easily. Even when you set rules for them, at times, they can lose their self-control and forget about those rules. That is why you need to work on improving your child's self-control, and this can be done by a few simple steps that we are going to discuss in this chapter. Showing any kind of bad behavior does not make your ADHD child bad. It is simply that they have problems with proper behavior.

Help Them Connect Their Behavior With Consequence

Kids who have ADHD cannot inhibit or delay their responses and this is a problem they deal with on a daily basis. They are always in the moment and not always in a good way. Sometimes they might act out without even giving the situation sufficient thought about whether they should have done it or not. The main reason behind this is that they cannot connect the consequences of their actions with the behavior that they are displaying. If someone has to make this connection, then they actually have to go through the process of taking a pause and thinking about their emotions and the events. They have to weigh in the consequences that will follow once they take action and then make a decision after considering everything.

This disconnect between consequence and behavior is a common occurrence among children who are suffering from ADHD. They cannot think clearly and often act out impulsively when things are happening all at once. They cannot remember any of the past references that can guide them in making the right decision. This is also why you will see that most ADHD children do not learn even after committing a mistake once. They are not able to see what is ahead of them in life because of problems and impairments in their memory. Moreover, it has been noticed that the concept of internal language develops much later in the life of ADHD kids. By internal language, I mean the voice that is present within all our heads that guides us and helps us regulate our behaviors.

So, you have to work together with your child and help them form a connection between the actions they take and the consequences that they have to face because of it. During their points of performance, you simply have to provide them with proper guidance, incentives, reminders, and cues, and you have to teach them that they have to do their best to meet the demands a particular situation poses in front of them instead of acting impulsively.

Whenever you see that your child is behaving in some improper way, you have to give them your feedback. Point out whatever is wrong in their behavior and then try to reinforce good behavior instead. And when they actually do something good, reward them. This will make the child understand that it is actually the kind of behavior you would want them to show, and the reward system will promote them towards such kind of behavior even more. In case they go off the track, you have to redirect them in a mild way and teach them that before they respond to something, they actually have to put the brakes and think whether it is appropriate behavior for that situation.

If you are able to teach all of this to your child the way you should, then you will also teach them how to be self-aware. Your child has to be in tune with everything that is going on, and only then can connect the consequence with their actions. And for this, they have to be self-aware. You have to develop a feedback system and it has to be consistent and immediate. If it is sparse, the child will not be able to form the connection.

Channelize Their Energy in Productive Things

ADHD kids often have this huge amount of energy with them that they don't know what to do with. When they don't get the right things to put their energy in, they vent it out at the wrong places. If you want to prevent it from happening, you have to give the kids something positive in which they can vent their energy. That's also why you need to include some physical activities in the routine of your ADHD kid. You can also play some games with them that would require investing some energy. Get activity boxes and spend quality time with your kids. There are certain games specially meant for ADHD kids that will boost their concentration too.

You can also make a list of chores for them that they have to complete, and in this way, they will stay busy. Problems with self-control also arise when your child is in school. You will learn more about it in the next chapter. You will often notice that when you tell your ADHD child to wait for something, they usually have a hard time waiting for things to happen. They get agitated and lose their calm. For example, if you give them two options and they have to choose one, like – if you tell them that they can have the larger cookie if they can wait but can have the smaller cookie right now, they will go for the option where they don't have to wait. But once you teach them how they can keep their energy under control and practice patience, things are going to become easier.

Work On Improving Their Listening Skills

One of the most important reasons why ADHD kids react before thinking is that they are not even listening properly. When your child knows the right moment to talk, and when they only have to listen, things can become easier. But more often than not, kids with ADHD don't realize this and this is what causes problems. It might sound easy to you that all they have to do is listen but it is not that easy in reality. This is because in order to brush up on their listening skills, ADHD kids have to wait for their turn to speak and like I already mentioned earlier, waiting is something they are not good at either.

Here are some ways in which you can help your child work on his/her listening skills –

- ☆ If you are explaining something to your child and you are not sure whether they are actually listening to you or whether they understood the whole thing or not, then you can ask them questions to be sure about it. Also, you have to be very clear with your instructions, and even then, there might be chances of your child not understanding what you said. That is why you should ask your child to repeat the instructions back to you and this will help you to figure out what they actually understood and what they didn't. Also, explain each step or instructions one after the other. Don't clump everything together. You should definitely use words like last or first in order to make the instructions even more structured and bring a sense of order.

- ☆ You should also keep your words predictable when you are talking to your child. Don't use too many new words and keep your conversations predictable. This is very important in order to increase the comprehending power of the child with respect to conversations. They will know that you are going to use these words, and this will make them feel calmer and secure.
- ☆ Use some movement while you talk. For example, you can use hand gestures, or you can even show something in action. All these strategies have been proven to be quite helpful when it comes to teaching ADHD kids.
- ☆ There are also some simple things that you can do to improve their listening skills like – when they are watching TV, you can sit beside them and ask them to explain to you what just happened. In this way, you will understand whether they were truly listening to the things on TV. Similarly, you can ask your child what did they talk about to some person on the phone and you have to ask this after they have just hung up the phone.

Teach Them to Follow Directions

As you already know that ADHD kids find it difficult to do the most basic things of life, one of them is following directions. There are a whole lot of skills involved in a child following your directions, as you said – listening, staying focused, and understanding what you said. All of these skills don't come easily to kids with ADHD. If you have noticed that when you tell your child multiple things to do but he/she remembers only a few, then they need to be taught how to follow directions. Once they learn this, they can also practice self-control.

If you want the child to comply with the directions you have given, you also have to ensure that you give them the right way. If you give instructions to your child while chatting or while doing dishes, they probably heard only some parts of it and understood none. There are so many distractions in their surroundings, the sound of the utensils clanking, the water from the tap flowing, and all of this probably is making him/her think about swimming in the pool in the summers. And then he/she is already lost in their world of thoughts thinking about last summer you all went on a vacation to the beach. That is why drawn-out directions are not going to help your child. They find it difficult to process what you said when you say a lot of things together. This creates frustration for both the child and the parent.

But if you want to make the directions clear and help your child to understand, then here are some steps that you can follow –

- ☆ You have to get the attention of your child, and that is why I would advise you to move closer to him and maybe put a hand on his shoulders or arm. In this way, they will stay somewhat connected to you.
- ☆ Never lose eye contact while giving directions to your child.
- ☆ The instructions should be actionable and simple. If you ask them to get ready for school, they don't know how to get ready for school. Instead, you have to clearly mention the steps – put on your fresh underwear, put on your shirt, put on your trousers/skirt, and so on.
- ☆ Your voice should be firm, and your words have to be clear.
- ☆ If there are any explanations that you have to give to your child, do that before you give the instructions. Explaining after the instructions might make them forget what they actually have to do.
- ☆ Once you have given all the instructions, don't leave immediately. Wait for a few minutes and see whether he/she is actually attentive and doing what you asked for or not. If you notice them doing what you asked, then you have to praise them at once, and they will feel even more motivated. But if you notice that they are doing it wrong, it is probably because they did not understand the instructions

clearly. So, you should make them understand one more time.

- ☆ In case your child is being stubborn and not complying to what you just said, you should implement some 'IF' and 'THEN' sentences, because this will give them an idea about the consequences that are going to come because of their actions. If they comply after this, you should acknowledge their effort and praise them. But if this doesn't work and they are not complying, then you have to create a loss of something as a consequence like a toy or some privilege like TV time.
- ☆ Your approach should be calm and at the same time – consistent too. But if it is only you in your family who are doing it in this way, then it is not going to work. So, you have to talk to other members of the family too and ensure that everyone is following the same method for giving directions.
- ☆ In the case of daily routines, you can make them a checklist to follow, and this will not only keep them on track but also allow them to work independently without anyone reminding them things.

Inculcate Problem-Solving Skills

Children with ADHD often seem to lose their calm when it comes to solving the problems of day-to-day life. If something is too difficult for them to deal with, they can even remain stuck in that one problem. They become overwhelmed, and they start thinking too much which brings about a sense of uncertainty. This is how they are not able to reach any sensible conclusion and that is why they get frustrated and act out. Moreover, the original issue gets lost amongst such overwhelming and confusing thoughts.

There are five very important steps that you have to teach your child so that solving problems becomes an easier task for them –

- ☆ Tell them to ask themselves – what the problem is.
- ☆ Then, ask them to think about any three possible solutions that they think might solve the problem.
- ☆ Ask them to think about each option for a minute or two and analyzing whether it would be a good solution or a bad one.
- ☆ After analyzing, tell them to pick one from the three solutions they thought of.
- ☆ Tell them to try out that option, and they will know whether it is going to work out or not.

You have to teach your kids to solve their own problems because that is how they are going to grow up and this is a process. It is not going to happen overnight, and you have to be patient with them. You also have to inculcate the values of self-reliance; otherwise, your child will not be able to depend on their own selves for solving the problem. If you think your child is displaying some behavior that is out of their control, don't punish them for that. But you also have to make them understand that once you become self-reliant, it does not mean that you will be barred from asking for help from others. In case they become stuck somewhere, they can always ask for help from people they know and trust.

In case your child is having difficulty finding solutions simply by thinking, ask them to write the solutions down. This is somewhat like brainstorming. In case they are having a mood, you have to teach them to say positive things to themselves which can help them control their mood. This is how they are going to practice self-control when you are not there in front of them to help them out. In short, teach them how they can give themselves a positive pep talk. Dealing with all of these things and inculcating good behaviors is like forming new habits and habit formation is not an easy task. You have to be consistent in order to make this process a success.

#6 Tips to Help You Child Overcome School Problems

Almost every child faces some kind of problem or the other in their schools, but the kids suffering from ADHD have this problem even more than the others. This is mainly because the major problem with ADHD is that the kids are not able to concentrate or maintain their attention on any single thing for a long time. And this is exactly something you need to do when you are in school. There will also be several other challenges for kids in school. Your kids are expected to follow rules. They are expected to stay neat and they are expected to get along well with other kids. In this chapter, we are going to discuss some of the common problems and how they can be dealt with both by parents and by teachers.

Improve Their Social Skills

The social skills aspect needs to be highly stressed once your child starts going to school. ADHD kids often face difficulties because they are not accepted within their peer groups so easily, and they are not good at making friends.

They are not able to show positivity while connecting with others because of their hyperactive and inattentive nature.

Here are some things that you can do in order to improve their social skills –

Increase Their Social Awareness

It has been noticed time and again that kids who are suffering from ADHD cannot monitor their own social behaviors that well – in simpler terms, they are not socially aware. They do not know how bad they can make others feel with the wrong actions, and they do not have a proper understanding of the behavior they should show in a social setting. In certain cases, they might even feel that when they interacted with a peer, it went well but in reality, it was not even close to well. Thus, they have problems in reading a situation correctly and thus they assess things the wrong way. That, in turn, leads to wrong self-evaluation. You have to teach these skills to your child directly.

Teach the Skills Required and Practice

No matter how many past experiences your child has, you will often notice that when a child is suffering from ADHD, they cannot really learn from the mistakes of their past. They do not think about consequences before reacting. That is why, whenever they display any kind of inappropriate behavior, you have to take the stand and give them feedback that it was not the right kind of behavior for that situation. One such way of doing so is engaging in role-playing activities of social settings. This is one of the best ways of teaching proper social skills to your child. You can also teach them how they can react to teasing in schools, which can otherwise be quite a difficult situation to handle for ADHD kids.

Don't try to do too many things at once. Start with only a few areas of problem so that your child does not feel overwhelmed with the process. For example, ADHD kids face a problem in starting conversations or even maintain one. So, you can teach them how reciprocity is maintained in conversations. Then, you can move on to how they can resolve conflicts in schools if they arise. You should also teach them to build certain boundaries in certain situations so that their personal space is not compromised. ADHD kids sometimes even face problems speaking in a normal voice, and so, you should teach them what a normal tone is and what is too loud. Once you have taught them these skills, you have to keep practicing with them over and over again so that this becomes the usual thing to them.

Work on Friendship Development

Everyone needs friends, and so do your ADHD kids but they face a lot of problems when it comes to making friends. One amazing of ensuring that your child develops some nice friendships is to send them on playdates. In this way, you can also teach them positive peer skills and they will also get a perfect opportunity where they can put those skills into action. But don't jump to group activities right in the beginning. You can set up play times for your child with another child or two. You should also keep in mind that the length of the playdate is a big factor here. ADHD kids don't do well in prolonged play dates.

If your child keeps on struggling with social interactions, the middle and high school period is going to become very tough on them. That is why you have to ensure that they have at least one good friend. This is because when they don't have any friends at all, this kind of social isolation can fuel them into moving in with the kids that might have a negative influence on them. This is very common in middle and high school.

You can even encourage your child to become a member of communities and groups where they can foster positive peer relationships. But whatever group you enlist them in, you have to make sure that the group leader knows about the ADHD and that he/she knows how to treat ADHD children.

Work With the School to Make the Peer Status Better

Problems can become worse for a child with ADHD once he/she has been labeled in some bad way by the peer group at school. The reputation remains with them for most of their lives and can make it difficult for them to go through their day-to-day lives. Encouraging your child towards social relationships will become harder once your child gets a negative reputation for something. For such reputational effects, it would be better if you reach out to the school and work together with the teacher or coaches.

It is important that you have a positive relationship with the teacher of your child. You have to inform them about ADHD and your child's interests and strengths. You have to let the teacher know about the major pain points of your child. If there are any strategies that you have seen particularly effective in the case of your child, you have to let the teacher know about them too.

When your child is still in kindergarten, it is natural for them to look up to their teacher when they cannot figure out whom to be friends with. If the teacher is able to redirect them in a gentle way with patience, acceptance, and warmth, then that child might be able to make friends. At least, the social status of the child can be improved with the teacher's help. The teachers can even find someone compassionate in class and pair your child up with that person so that your child gets social acceptance.

In order to improve the environment in the classroom and make it friendly to your child, you have to work together with the teacher.

How Can Teachers Increase Social Competencies?

Your child meets the teacher every day in school, and it is the teacher who is responsible for regulating the behavior of the students in the class and so, there are certain things that the teacher can do in order to increase social competencies:

- ☆ You can teach them the right skills to enhance student awareness. You have to give them positive attention and show them what pro-social behavior means. This has to be done not only in the classroom setting but also outside the classroom setting.
- ☆ When the child does something wrong, you have to correct them by providing them feedback, but the feedback shouldn't be embarrassing or judgmental. Your main aim should be on building positive social skills of the child.
- ☆ When you find that one particular child is too weak in the social skills part, you can pair them up in groups that are supportive

and will not tease the child. Kids who are socially isolated have to be helped out in terms of friendships. You have to facilitate friendships for these kids.

- ☆ When the kids engage in cooperative behavior, take their photos, and then hang those group activity photos in places that can be easily seen in the classroom, and this will encourage positivity.

Expectations and Rules Must Be Realistic

If you want your child to do well in school and meet success, you have to be realistic about both your expectations and the rules they have to follow. The developmental delay in kids with ADHD is a very big factor that should be taken into consideration when both parents and teachers are forming the rules for them. The child's challenges have to be accommodated, and that is how these rules should be made.

The major difficulties of ADHD kids that have to be kept in mind while setting rules and expectations are as follows –

- ☆ Problems in following directions or remembering routines or steps that they were asked to follow
- ☆ Recalling any instructions that were given to them in order to complete a task

- ☆ Understanding what to do through observation alone
- ☆ Regulation of emotions
- ☆ Time management
- ☆ Distractions and once distracted, finding their way back to the point of discussion
- ☆ Navigating around the problems that arise in their way

But here are some ways in which you can keep the expectations and rules realistic and predictable for an ADHD kid –

- ☆ Implementation of hands-on teaching techniques and the usage of very simple language
- ☆ In order to make the child succeed despite the challenges, you can manipulate the time sometimes. Also, you can avoid any hectic tasks to the ADHD kid right away in the morning so that their energy is not drained at the beginning of the day. You can also wait until the effect of the ADHD medication kicks in before you urge them to keep following the routine.
- ☆ In order to make the tasks easier, you can provide them with worksheets that will give them visual support and clearly show them the steps that they have to follow. In this way, they can achieve even a very complex goal. You also have to order the steps properly otherwise, the child can get

lost in thoughts figuring out which task to do first.

- ☆ You can provide them with gentle redirection or prompts when they start losing their way.
- ☆ If you want them not to lose track of time, you should provide them with some visual timers.
- ☆ Establish an incentive program so that it promotes the good behavior of the child.
- ☆ Positive enforcement and expectations have to be consistent.
- ☆ In case the child is anxious or sad, listen to what he/she has to say and empathize with them. In this way, they will feel understood and heard, and their emotions will calm down.
- ☆ In case things don't go as planned, you have to acknowledge it in front of the child that it's okay if sometimes things don't turn out to be the way they thoughts because there are a lot of circumstances at play and they might override the rules and expectations.
- ☆ If you are rewarding the child for good behavior, be consistent with that too; otherwise, the child will not understand what you want and will get mixed messages.

Manage Their Distractibility

Distraction is something that every ADHD child has to battle with, and when they are in school, this distraction has to be handled by the teachers. This is because when they are distracted, they are not taking in any of the classroom information because their mind is somewhere else. If the task at hand requires a lot of mental effort, then the distractions become even stronger. At times, you might feel that the child is listening to you when in reality, they are not. They are simply pretending to listen to you but they cannot really retain the information. Anything starting from a bird chirping in the nearby trees or someone passing through the corridor beside the classroom can distract the child.

So, some of the things that you can do are that you should never allow too long periods of work. Instead, you can try breaking down those periods into small chunks. There are so many other strategies too which involve increasing movement and physical placement and I am going to list them below –

- ☆ Ensure that the child is not seated anywhere where there are windows and doors located close by. If you want to keep the child focused at home, then you also have to make sure that the pets are not in the room while your child is trying to focus on something.

- ☆ Never conduct seated activities for too long. You can alternate the times with those activities that require the child to move around the room or show at least some form of physical movement.
- ☆ All the necessary and important information must be given to the child in written format, and you should also stick a to-do list or a checklist for the day when the child can notice easily – for example, the class bulletin board. You should also remind the child from time to time that you have put up the necessary information on the bulletin board.
- ☆ If there are any big assignments that have to be completed today, you can divide it into smaller chunks, and when the kids have completed one task, you can give them a short break before they start the next task.

Reduce Any Kind of Interruptions

Like I already told you multiple times, kids who suffer from ADHD face problems in controlling their impulses, and thus, you might notice that these kids will speak out of turn while you are teaching something. This is noticed at home too when the kids start speaking when they should not. Sometimes, what they say might not be something normal and be somewhat like an outburst. In fact, in some cases, these outbursts can be quite rude or even aggressive. This, in turn, creates a lot of extra problems for the kid in the classroom, and they are not able to socialize with anyone.

Moreover, kids with ADHD have very fragile self-esteem which makes things worse. If you point out that they are being undisciplined or behaving in a way that they shouldn't and if you do this in front of the whole class, they might take it to hurt and situations can go completely out of control. That is why you need to develop a kind of talk that only you and the child will understand – somewhat like a 'secret language.' It doesn't always have to be verbal. You can do it with the help of gestures too. As long as you can communicate to the child that they are causing an unnecessary interruption, but in a discreet manner, it should be fine. On the contrary, when you are able to take a class free of any kind of interruptions, you should praise the child.

Manage Their Impulsivity

When some difficult social situations arise, you will often see that ADHD kids are acting out, and they are not thinking before saying or doing things. This is exactly what is known as trouble with impulse control. This is also why ADHD kids are labeled as unruly or rude. And this problem with impulsivity can create a lot of problems for the childwhen he/she is in school. But you can impose some behavior plans and make them feel that they have control over the day, to avoid this feeling of being insecure that is the root cause of impulsivity.

Here are some things that you can do:

- ☆ Like I said before, written things have more impact on kids with ADHD than verbal instructions. So, you should write down a very specific behavioral plan for the child and then attach it to their desk.
- ☆ Whenever you notice any kind of misbehavior from the child's side, you have to clearly state the consequences of their behavior. In order to make the child realize that what they did was an act of misbehavior, you have to be as detailed as possible while stating the consequences.
- ☆ When the child displaysgood behavior, don't just praise them in private, praise them out loud in front of everyone. This will give them a clear idea of what is wrong and what is right.
- ☆ You should also write down the schedule of the day, and whenever the child completes something, practice crossing off the item from the list and this will impart of sense of control to the child, which, in turn, will make him/her feel calmer.

Manage Hyperactivity

You will notice that whenever a child is suffering from ADHD, they have this tendency to be constant in motion. They might be fidgeting, fighting with other kids, twist things, kick things, or simply show some kind of movement. There are several creative ways in which you can help achild manage his/her hyperactivity. When you teach the child different ways in which they can channelize their energy, they can actually remain focused when they are doing some work. This release of energy is of absolute necessity if you want the child to calm down.

Here are some strategies to follow:

- ☆ You can send the child on an errand. You can give them some tasks that they can complete for you. It can be something as simple as sharpening a few pencils, and for that, they have to go across the room to sharpen them. You can ask them to distribute some sheets to the rest of the class or you can also ask them to bring some chalks from the office.
- ☆ Another way in which you can manage their hyperactivity is by encouraging them to engage in some kind of sport. This can be simply running too. You should also make sure that the child is not skipping on the Physical Education classes.

- ☆ As a parent, you can limit their time spent on the TV so that they can actually spend more time playing outside, which is also a type of physical activity. This will prevent them from being hyperactive in school.
- ☆ You can give them a stress ball or any other stress-relieving object that they can press and squeeze. This can be done even when they are seated in the class. But this stress ball or toy can prevent any other symptoms of their hyperactive nature since they are releasing their energy by squeezing it.

Make Learning Fun

If you want to make a child attentive towards their study and encourage them to learn more things, you have to make the process fun for them. You can provide them with some interesting trivia, or play some funny videos which are actually teaching them something, or you can even make some silly songs that will help them remember stuff from boring subjects.

Mathematical concepts are one of the most difficult things to inculcate in a child who is suffering from ADHD. That is why you can use games to make the process fun and here are some ideas for you –

- ☆ There are so many games that you can play. In order to make numbers fun, you can use dominoes, dice, or even memory cards. If you don't have access to these, don't worry, there are so many other ways which don't require anything. For example, you can use your toes and fingers and tuck them in while you are subtracting or adding.

- ☆ If you are solving some word problems with the child, why not draw some pictures that make the process interesting? Mathematical concepts can be understood very easily when you illustrate the things for your child. If the math problem says that you had ten apples, why not draw ten apples on the board and encourage the child to draw them too?
- ☆ If there is a big word or phrase that your child has to remember, then you can invest some acronyms for them that are funny. In this way, they will remember the order of words too.

The next thing to teach an ADHD child is to read properly. It can be a tough task too, because ADHD kids are often not able to stay focused on any one thing for a long period of time. Start by giving them some interesting factual books or stories so that they are actually interested in reading them.

Some things that you can do to make the process easier are –

- ☆ You can read to the kids as a parent, and this will also allow you to spend some quality time with them.
- ☆ While reading, you can ask the child about what he/she thinks is going to happen next.
- ☆ You can even try and act the story out to make the process even more fun. Make some nice costumes and use funny voices.

You should also encourage your child to do homework in the right way. But for that, you should also make them organized by color-coding subjects so that they do not become overwhelmed with the amount of homework that they have to do. Don't make them do home works for a long duration of time. If they have been at it for about twenty minutes, give them a break of ten minutes.

Sometimes breaks that involve going to the bathroom or sipping water or their favorite milkshake also boost the process of studying.

Learning to Manage ADHD Behavior Outside of School

Your child cannot always stay at home, and there are a lot of other places where they have to go other than school and you have to teach them how they can manage their ADHD behavior in those places as well. This chapter will especially be useful to parents who are thinking of going on a trip with your child who suffers from ADHD.

Car Travel

Traveling by car is something that most kids suffering from ADHD dread. It can be quite a challenge for parents too. The main reason behind this is that children who are victims of ADHD usually prefer to stay in their routines, and their sense of order is easily damaged by things like long car rides. And this can easily lead to a phase of turmoil and tantrums. The end result of this is that the entire family finds it difficult to travel by car anymore. But I am going to give you some small suggestions that can make your car travel better the next time –

☆ If you are going to take your child somewhere that involved riding the car, you have to prepare them mentally from a couple of days ahead. You cannot simply wake up one morning and tell them that you are going somewhere that involves staying in the car for five hours. You have to prepare them for the change of routine and scenery that is about to come. If you want to make them feel at home even when they are traveling by car, you have to take their suggestions on what they want to bring with them. You should also explain to them what this short trip is going to be about or where you are going or how the road is going to be so that they know what to expect and in this way, they will be mentally prepared for it.

☆ If the car travel is for a long time, your child might want to take a small nap in the car, but they are so used to sleeping in their own bed that the car will seem odd to them. That is it would be a good idea to bring their favorite stuffed toy or their favorite blanket so they can feel comfortable. The sense of familiarity can make them feel secure.

☆ Maintain at least some parts of the routine on the day of travel. For example, try to stick to the same time of waking up. If you wake your child up about one hour before their usual time, their mood might not be good, and they will be throwing even more tantrums. So, avoid scheduling trips that are too much off the usual routine of your child.

- ☆ If your child looks exhausted after a point of time, take a break and stop somewhere. When your child does not have a proper amount of sleep, the symptoms can start worsening, and you cannot let that happen especially when you are outside. So, make sure you encourage them to take small naps if you have been out for a long time or if you still have a long way to go.

- ☆ Don't change the behavioral rules. You have to make your child realize that simply because you are no longer at home and going somewhere in a car does not give them a free pass to do whatever they want. If they are misbehaving, make sure you remind them of the consequences.

- ☆ You also have to maintain your kid's social etiquette when you are outside. You can give him/her gentle reminders and follow the same process of reminding the consequences if they behave rudely.

- ☆ There are so many simple things that matter when you are going somewhere with your child in a car. They might not comply with your request or putting on the seatbelt. And if they are not listening to you, don't jump to the system of reminding them of the consequence right away. Instead, try to understand why your child is acting so grumpy. To keep your child cheerful, you can involve them in conversations that you are having.

☆ Another very common commotion that kids have while traveling in a car is regarding the seating arrangement. Sometimes, kids have a special preference for seating, and they get moody when they are not allowed to sit in that particular place. You have to teach them how to share and maintain a mutually agreed seating arrangement.

☆ Lastly, another very common problem that arises on trips is the part when you have to go to the bathroom. If your car trip is long, then it is quite natural for you to want to go to the bathroom. At first, your child might say that they will go to the bathroom when you want to go, but soon after that, they might throw tantrums about going to the bathroom right away. That is why you have to take the responsibility of taking your child to the bathroom before you leave so that they don't have to go anytime soon. And even if they want to go after a few minutes, remind them that it is difficult to find a toilet on the road and so, they have to wait for a few more minutes or hours depending on the road and availability of bathrooms.

Resolving Misbehavior in Public Places

Are you always worried about what tantrum your ADHD child is going to throw whenever you walk into a store with them? Behavior is a very big issue with ADHD kids and whenever you ask them to do something that they don't want to, they might lash out at you. Whenever ADHD kids are overpowered with strong emotions, they usually cannot deal with it until and unless they act out or show an emotional outburst. But you have to do something about their misbehavior now otherwise, if you neglect it and let it foster then after a period of time, your child might develop ODD or oppositional defiant disorder. In fact, ODD has been found in as much as 40% of kids who are already suffering from ADHD.

Why Do Kids Act Out?

Before we go into how you can manage behavioral problems in ADHD kids, you have to understand why they act out. Think about their history of ADHD and how they have been dealing with it since childhood. It has been noticed that kids with ADHD have a tendency to be attracted to those things which they should be attracted to.

For example, if you tell them not to behave badly, they will be attracted to malicious intent. That is why, when you are outside, and you ask them to remain seated, they will run around the restaurant or speak too loudly. And all of this can make you stressed out in public places.

It is also these situations that lead to negative interactions between you and your child. When you keep telling the child from very early in their childhood that this behavior is wrong and that they should not do it, the kid starts thinking that there is something wrong with them and so they start internalizing all their feelings. And at times, they start acting out towards those who are actually asking them not to do such things.

Why Do Kids With ADHD Throw Tantrums?

In the previous section, I gave you an explanation as to why kids act out, and now we are going to see why they throw tantrums. Kids who are suffering from ADHD have to usually put in a lot of effort into tasks that seem boring or are repetitive. This means that they have to fight a lot of resistance which automatically makes the task even more challenging. And if the task is not allowing them to do something that they like, for example, watching TV, then they are not going to do that task at all and turn it into a battleground. These are basically avoidance strategies that your kids are using, but for you, they quickly become power struggles and acts of defiance.

Also, when they start throwing such tantrums, most parents change the conditions of the task so that it becomes easier for them, and this makes the child think that they can throw tantrums whenever they feel like and keep reducing things like this.

What Strategies to Use?

Now, let us see how you can keep such behaviors under control. All the disciplinary strategies that are usually used with other kids might not work with kids suffering from ADHD because of one single reason, and that is, you have already developed a kind of negative interaction with the kid. Also, if you want the strategies to work out in the best way possible, you have to stop losing your temper. If you have a child who does not show bad behavior too often, then speaking to them firmly or raising your voice might actually bring them back on track.

But the problem lies with the kids who have made it a habit to misbehave. If you keep shouting at them or raise your voice while you talk, they simply assume that to be normal and so they stop paying any kind of attention at all. Moreover, when you give too much punishment, the effectiveness of it all disappears. There are living in a world that is a perpetual state of punishment, and so it somehow loses its meaning. They don't find it a big deal even if they are punished one more time.

But here are some things that will work if you implement them correctly –

- ☆ When you are successful in bringing more structure to the life of kids suffering from ADHD, it has been noticed that they get quite some benefit from it. This means that you have to leave a clear set of instructions for them whenever you want them to do something. You have to note down exactly what you are expecting from them so that they are aware of it. If you don't help your child understand which behaviors are acceptable and which behaviors are not, how can they separate the right from the wrong?
- ☆ You have to build a positive relationship with your child. It is even more important if you want to correct the disruptive behavior of your child. This is because when the relationship between the parent and the child is not good and is mostly negative, then these disruptive behaviors tend to escalate.
- ☆ There is a term that is designated to this, and it is called scaffolding. If a child is facing behavioral problems, then in order to regulate that behavior, they require a proper family environment. If you want

your kids to learn something good, then you also have to provide them with a structure to do so.

- ☆ One of the most important reasons for bad behavior is that children are not able to regulate their emotions. And so, you need to work on making them more aware of their emotions and teach them how to practice self-control. I have already covered that in Chapter 5.

Help Them Deal With Group Situations

There will be several situations where your child will have to work together in a group. It can be in school or even at a party or when he/she goes out to play with others. But navigating such group situations is something that ADHD kids face trouble with. In fact, if care is not taken properly, then the situation will quickly escalate, and the entire group exercise will place a negative impact on your child. Just like any other child, if someone has ADHD, it does not inhibit them from wanting to make friends, or succeed in life or participate in group activities. Here are some of the things that you can do to help –

- ☆ Although most parents are aware that ADHD is actually a genuine disorder and has to be dealt with care, there are still some parents who do not believe in its existence. You have to make yourself understand that having ADHD is not the result of your upbringing. It is a brain disorder, and it definitely does not reflect your kid's intelligence. When you think that ADHD is not serious, you might take the tantrums and poor behavior of your child as willful, and then it can make matters worse.

- ☆ In order to deal with the high amount of energy that your child seems to possess, you have to encourage them to engage in different positive opportunities where they can spend this energy. When you try to make your child channelize their energy into something positive, it is even less likely for them to act out or misbehave.
- ☆ You have to establish a routine before switching gears. If you are going to take things to the next level in the group activity, give the child enough time to prepare for it.
- ☆ Sometimes, you will see that the child is acting out, but they don't really mean most of the things they say. It is just that their level of self-control is low but that doesn't mean they want to hurt you emotionally. So, your reaction to anything should be calm. You should not be acting immediately to retaliate with some form of punishment.
- ☆ There are certain correction strategies that you should use because it will help the child with the group activities. You should

not criticize anything they do. When they are finally taking the steps in the right direction, you should appreciate them instead of telling them how they can make it more perfect. Stop pushing them towards perfectionism because they don't have to be perfect. They simply have to keep doing what they are doing.

- ☆ Don't just focus on the negatives – like if you keep telling them what not to do, they will feel restrictive, but if you also tell them what they should do, then you are promoting positive activity in them.
- ☆ Refrain from accusing the child of anything. You have to accept the fact that they are a slow learner and you have to give them all the time they need. If you want to shape positive and good behavior in the child, then you should praise them whenever you catch them displaying good behavior.
- ☆ In case the child has been harnessing negative energy, you can ask them to perform some simple chores so that this negative energy doesn't accumulate in their body.

Yes, it's true that going out with your ADHD child can be a challenging task, especially because their mood keeps changing throughout the day. They can be extremely happy now and yet become sad in the next few hours. They also have a very low tolerance level to most things, and that is why they become frustrated very easily. But if you follow the steps that have been mentioned in this chapter, you will learn to slowly navigate through the situation.

Final Tips for Parenting a Child With ADHD

Throughout this book, I have discussed the various challenges that your child can face if he/she is suffering from ADHD, and I have also given the solutions to those problems. The process is definitely overwhelming and can even get frustrating at times. But since you are the parent, you have to take the responsibility of teaching your child how they can navigate through these issues and overcome all the challenges that they have to face daily. Also, the earlier you recognize these problems and address them, the happier your child will be later in their life.

Make It Interesting

Distraction is one of the most common enemies of anyone suffering from ADHD. Even the smallest of things can make them distracted. But in some cases, a child becomes way too focused on the task you give them, and this nature is called being hyper-focused. If you want your child to not get distracted and maintain their focus on the task at hand, the task should not be boring. Even if the text is boring, you have to make sure that you implement drawings or other visual things to make them feel interested about the topic that you are discussing.

Work On Their Organizational Skills

ADHD kids often have things cluttered, and this, in turn, creates a greater amount of confusion in them which can also make them feel overwhelmed. That is why staying organized is so important. This is even more important if you want your kids to study properly and finish their homework on time.

I am listing some things here that will help you in keeping your child's things organized –

- ☆ Pocket folders of different colors are very helpful. For example, in one folder (suppose the red-colored one), you can keep all the homework assignments. Another folder can be made for papers that have already been graded and returned. If the child has a lot of subjects, then you can create different folders for different subjects to make things easier.
- ☆ You can use the color-coded folders to separate the tasks that they still have to do and the tasks that they have already completed.

The study desk of your child also has to remain organized in order to make them willing to study. You can help your child clean the clutter and transform the table into a minimal one. You should also keep a basket beside the desk where your child can throw in all those items that they do not need. This basket should be kept beside the table at all times so that whenever your child comes across something they don't need, they can throw it out immediately. Here are some strategies to follow to make the study desk better and to encourage our child to study –

- ☆ You should select a place which has a fresh vibe and has a lot of natural lighting. This location should also be comfortable for your child with as low distractions as possible.
- ☆ The working surface should be free of any clutter. If you notice anything that is supposed to be thrown into the bin but has not been thrown yet, throw it away so that your child gets more space to study.
- ☆ Make your child clear the desks and shelves after regular intervals of days so that there doesn't remain any old paperwork or clutter.
- ☆ There should be sufficient storage space in the desk so that your child does not have to store the things here and there.
- ☆ Spend time with your child while you ask them to organize their room. You can make it a fun activity by doing it together.

Teach Them Time Management

ADHD kids seem to take forever for doing even the simplest tasks in their day-to-day life, and this is something you have to work on improving as a parent. If you try to make them do these tasks forcefully thinking that it is the solution, then you are doing it wrong because enforcing something on them is only going to aggravate the problem. Once you teach your kids how to manage their time, everything in their life is going to become more manageable, and navigating through the symptoms of ADHD will become simpler for them.

- ☆ I cannot stress enough about the importance of routines in the day-to-day life of ADHD kids. A fixed routine can solve a lot of problems in their life. You have to first think about all the responsibilities they have and then sit down with them and make the routine. But remember that you cannot make the routine entirely about the tasks that you want them to complete. There should be enough time for activities and sufficient breaks in between. Also, you have to keep some sameness as to if you are scheduling playtime at 4 pm on Monday, make sure it is at 4 pm on Tuesday too. This will give structure to the lives of ADHD kids.
- ☆ You have to work on eliminating any kind of dawdling. Keep checking on them to

prevent such incidences. You have to stick to the times that you have fixed for each activity, and if you want, you can practice using a timer to enforce those times. To encourage positive behavior, an incentive-based program is also a very good idea.

Remind Yourself That Every Child Misbehaves

With all the challenges that come your way while handling your ADHD child, it is very easy to be lost in the flow. You have to know and remind yourself that ADHD is not responsible for all types of bad behaviors. And if you think that everything that your child does is because of ADHD, then it will let them get away with a lot of things just because they have ADHD. That is why it is important to remind yourself that sometimes children misbehave and not everything has to be managed. Yes, there are certain behaviors that cannot be neglected, but at the end of the day, you have to figure out which of the behaviors should be managed, and which of them can be dealt with some other day.

Be Calm

Dealing with all the chaos yourself, your internal balance might get affected and you might not be feeling well. That is why it is advised to all parents that you need to stay calm yourself if you want to handle your ADHD kid in the right way. When your brain is calm and is able to think clearly, it can solve problems even more easily and can also make communications in a better way. You will be facing challenging situations on an everyday basis and here are some strategies to implement if you want to remain calm through all of it –

- ☆ Practice yoga
- ☆ Meditate regularly
- ☆ Walk in a calming outdoor space or nature
- ☆ Don't worry too much about what is going to happen next
- ☆ Reduce the consumption of alcohol or caffeine

Approach a Specialist for Support

If you are facing too much stress dealing with your ADHD child all by yourself, then it is time that you take the help of a specialist. There are so many support groups that you can approach apart from professional help. But choosing the specialist is also going to be a major task. The specialist you choose for your child should be someone with whom they are comfortable. You can start by taking recommendations from the primary doctor of your child and then go for an appointment with the specialist to see whether your child likes him/her. Before you find the right fit, you might have to go to several of them, and that is completely fine. Don't settle for anything else because if the specialist is not right, then your child will not be able to talk to them openly, and a true relationship cannot be established ever.

Other Adults Are Not Your Enemy

Parents of ADHD kids are usually very protective and in doing so, they sometimes become too protective and think of other adults as their enemy. But it is not so. You might feel that others in your family or other adults surrounding your child are not giving him/her the care they need but you have to understand that everyone has their own way of caring. But if you strongly feel that someone is not giving the care they should, you should indulge in a good form of communication rather than treating the other person as your enemy. You can talk to them about your child, tell them about his/her strengths and weakness, or what their preferences are. You can tell them about what you feel is the most fruitful way of addressing the challenging behavior of your child.

Pick Your Battles Wisely

When you are with your child who is very hyperactive most of the time and shows impulsive behavior, it can automatically lead to a power struggle. This becomes even more difficult when it is something that you have to endure every day. In that case, you simply have to learn to pick your battles. You cannot answer every small tantrum thrown by your child; otherwise, you will become frustrated, and the day is going to become even more stressful. So, in order to alleviate your stress, you have to learn how you can let certain small things go so that you can put your focus on other things which are more important than that.

Encourage Your Child to Exercise

I have told you in previous chapters as well that it is important for kids with ADHD to burn off the extra energy in their body in some positive way; otherwise, they will not be able to focus on important tasks and give in to hyperactive attitude. Also, when you promote exercise, you are actually preventing the chances of any kind of anxiety or depression in your child. There is another benefit of proper exercise and that is – it helps in maintaining healthy sleep patterns. In fact, when your child exercises regularly, it even stimulates their brain to perform better. So, you can keep skipping ropes and balls at home. This will ensure that your child can engage in physical activities even if they don't want to socialize in a group.

In most cases, ADHD children tend to develop good habits with respect to staying physically active when their parents are a good role model. That's why you should encourage some weekend outdoor activities where all of you can enjoy together, or you can even go for hikes to nearby places.

Don't Command But Explain

ADHD kids don't do well with commands and so that should be the last resort. If you ask your child to do something, it is most likely that they will ask you the reason behind it and so you should explain the reason to them. Of course, some things are not age-appropriate, and so you have to explain to them things that you think can be explained. In this way, your child will no longer remain confused about why they are doing what they are doing. Their worries will be addressed. Make sure you use completely clear language and positive words when you do the explaining.

Also, when you take the time out to explain things to your child, they feel that you respect them and this feeling itself promotes them to follow your directions.

Don't Use Negative Words

It is important to dwell on positivity while handling a child with ADHD. You should give feedbacks but give them in a positive manner so that your child's level of confidence increases. If you keep making them feel that whatever they do is wrong, then they will start feeling that no one loves them. This makes the outbursts worse and sometimes even out of control. The usage of any form of negative language is bad for a child with ADHD or for any child for that matter.

I know that at times, it might seem impossible for you to enforce positivity and that is why you, as a parent, should always have an outlet where you can express your worries or concerns. This can be someone you know like your spouse, mother, father, friend, or even a therapist. You will even find some groups for parents of ADHD children both online and offline and you can interact with those group members too because they face similar challenges like you on a daily basis.

Conclusion

Thank you for making it through to the end of *ADHD - Tools for Kids*, let's hope it was informative and able to provide you with all of the tools you need to achieve your goals whatever they may be.

All the solutions that I have given in this book aim at one single thing, and that is to help you teach your child how to engage in effective self-care and self-control in all situations despite their ADHD. This is important for dealing with their present and also for having a healthy future. If you follow the strategies in the right way, you will also be building a special bond with your child, where you will both have respect for each other. Don't stress too much. Just stay calm and implement what you have learned and things will start falling into place.

Kids with ADHD already go through a lot of stress in their day-to-day lives, trying to cope with everything that goes on around them. But if you follow the strategies mentioned in this book, you can make their daily struggle a bit easier. Kids will have a problem being organized, remembering stuff, or even doing the most basic things of life. But you cannot leave hope. You have to keep faith in them and take it one day at a time. The symptoms of ADHD are different for every child. Some of them might act grouchy in the morning while some of them might be too moody in the evenings. You have to monitor your child's symptoms and think about how you can make the hardest days in your child's life a bit easier.

Finally, if you found this book useful in anyway, a review on Amazon is always appreciated!

Other books by Angie Turner

Dyslexia - tools for kids

Dyslexia isn't a disease, it's not a problem, it's just a different way of learning and with the right tools, everyone can reach great goals!

In "Dyslexia tools for kids" you can find:

- *How dyslexic children learn*
- *What are their difficulties*
- *Find the right method to study*
- *How to set up winning daily strategies*

Learn about dyslexia and help your child overcome his difficulties!

www.amazon.com/dp/B088C4C4VY

Made in United States
Orlando, FL
13 March 2023

30982289R00067